50 Lazy Keto Recipes

By: Kelly Johnson

Table of Contents

- Bacon and Egg Cups
- Cheesy Cauliflower Rice
- Keto Taco Bowls
- Sausage and Cabbage Skillet
- Avocado Tuna Salad
- Ham and Cheese Roll-Ups
- Egg Salad Lettuce Wraps
- Keto Pizza Chaffles
- Cream Cheese Scrambled Eggs
- Ground Beef and Zucchini Skillet
- BLT Lettuce Wraps
- Chicken Alfredo Bake
- Zoodle Spaghetti with Meat Sauce
- Broccoli Cheese Soup
- Cauliflower Mac and Cheese
- Keto Cheeseburger Casserole
- Buffalo Chicken Lettuce Wraps

- Bunless Bacon Cheeseburgers
- Taco-Stuffed Avocados
- Pepperoni Pizza Zucchini Boats
- Egg Roll in a Bowl
- Keto Chicken Salad
- Garlic Butter Shrimp
- Keto Sloppy Joes
- Pork Chop and Green Beans Skillet
- Keto Tuna Melt
- Chicken Fajita Bowl
- Creamy Spinach-Stuffed Chicken
- Keto Egg Muffins
- Mushroom and Swiss Omelet
- Hot Dog Lettuce Wraps
- Chicken Bacon Ranch Casserole
- Keto Meatballs
- Shrimp and Broccoli Stir-Fry
- Keto Quesadillas (cheese shell)
- Pepperoni Cheese Crisps

- Sausage Egg Casserole
- Cobb Salad
- Keto Chicken Nuggets
- Cauliflower Tots
- Chili Dog Casserole
- Pulled Pork Lettuce Wraps
- Greek Salad with Grilled Chicken
- Keto Chicken Stir-Fry
- Philly Cheesesteak Stuffed Peppers
- Bacon-Wrapped Asparagus
- Turkey and Cheese Roll-Ups
- Keto Deviled Eggs
- Spinach and Feta Stuffed Chicken
- Caprese Chicken Skillet

Bacon and Egg Cups

Ingredients:

- 6 slices bacon
- 6 large eggs
- Salt and pepper to taste
- Fresh herbs for garnish (optional)

Instructions:

1. Preheat oven to 375°F (190°C).
2. Line a muffin tin with a slice of bacon in each cup, forming a circle along the edge.
3. Crack an egg into each bacon-lined muffin cup.
4. Season with salt and pepper.
5. Bake for 12–15 minutes, or until eggs are set to your liking.
6. Garnish with fresh herbs if desired, and serve warm.

Cheesy Cauliflower Rice

Ingredients:

- 1 medium cauliflower, grated or riced
- 1 tbsp butter
- 1 cup shredded cheddar cheese
- ¼ cup heavy cream
- Salt and pepper to taste
- Chopped parsley for garnish (optional)

Instructions:

1. Heat butter in a skillet over medium heat.
2. Add the riced cauliflower and sauté for 5–7 minutes until tender.
3. Stir in heavy cream and shredded cheese, cooking until the cheese is melted and the mixture is creamy.
4. Season with salt and pepper.
5. Garnish with chopped parsley if desired, and serve warm.

Keto Taco Bowls

Ingredients:

- 1 lb ground beef
- 1 packet taco seasoning (or homemade seasoning)
- 1 cup cauliflower rice
- 1 avocado, diced
- ¼ cup shredded cheese (cheddar, Mexican blend, or your choice)
- 1 tbsp sour cream
- Salsa (optional)
- Fresh cilantro for garnish (optional)

Instructions:

1. Cook ground beef in a skillet over medium heat until browned, stirring in taco seasoning and a little water to help coat the meat.
2. Meanwhile, prepare cauliflower rice in a separate skillet, cooking for 5–7 minutes until tender.
3. Assemble bowls with a layer of cauliflower rice, followed by seasoned beef, cheese, avocado, and sour cream.
4. Top with salsa and fresh cilantro for added flavor, and serve.

Sausage and Cabbage Skillet

Ingredients:

- 1 lb sausage (Italian, breakfast, or your favorite type)
- 1 medium head of cabbage, shredded
- 1 onion, chopped
- 2 cloves garlic, minced
- 2 tbsp olive oil
- Salt and pepper to taste

Instructions:

1. Heat olive oil in a large skillet over medium heat.
2. Add sausage and cook until browned and cooked through, breaking it apart as it cooks.
3. Remove sausage from the pan and set aside.
4. In the same pan, sauté onion and garlic until softened, about 3–4 minutes.
5. Add shredded cabbage to the pan and cook for 5–7 minutes, stirring occasionally, until the cabbage is tender.
6. Return sausage to the pan and mix everything together.
7. Season with salt and pepper, then serve hot.

Avocado Tuna Salad

Ingredients:

- 1 can tuna, drained
- 1 ripe avocado, mashed
- 2 tbsp mayonnaise
- 1 tbsp lemon juice
- 1 stalk celery, finely chopped
- Salt and pepper to taste
- Fresh parsley for garnish (optional)

Instructions:

1. In a bowl, combine tuna, mashed avocado, mayonnaise, lemon juice, and chopped celery.
2. Mix everything together until creamy and well-combined.
3. Season with salt and pepper to taste.
4. Garnish with fresh parsley if desired, and serve with lettuce wraps or on its own.

Ham and Cheese Roll-Ups

Ingredients:

- 8 slices of deli ham
- 4 oz cream cheese, softened
- ½ cup shredded cheddar cheese
- 1 tbsp Dijon mustard (optional)
- Fresh herbs for garnish (optional)

Instructions:

1. Spread a thin layer of cream cheese on each slice of ham.
2. Add a sprinkle of shredded cheddar cheese and a dab of Dijon mustard, if desired.
3. Roll up each slice of ham into a tight cylinder.
4. Serve as is or chill for 15 minutes for extra firmness.
5. Garnish with fresh herbs if desired and serve.

Egg Salad Lettuce Wraps

Ingredients:

- 4 large eggs, hard-boiled and chopped
- 2 tbsp mayonnaise
- 1 tsp mustard
- 1 tbsp chopped celery (optional)
- Salt and pepper to taste
- 4 large lettuce leaves (romaine or butter lettuce)

Instructions:

1. In a bowl, mix chopped eggs, mayonnaise, mustard, celery, salt, and pepper until well combined.
2. Spoon the egg salad mixture onto each lettuce leaf.
3. Fold the edges of the lettuce over the filling to create a wrap.
4. Serve immediately or refrigerate for later.

Keto Pizza Chaffles

Ingredients:

- 1 large egg
- ½ cup shredded mozzarella cheese
- 2 tbsp almond flour
- 1 tsp Italian seasoning
- 1 tbsp grated Parmesan cheese
- 2 tbsp pizza sauce (low-carb)
- 10–12 pepperoni slices (optional)

Instructions:

1. Preheat a waffle maker.
2. In a bowl, whisk together egg, mozzarella, almond flour, Italian seasoning, and Parmesan.
3. Pour the mixture into the waffle maker and cook until golden and crispy (about 3–4 minutes).
4. Once cooked, top each chaffle with a spoonful of pizza sauce and pepperoni slices.
5. Serve immediately as a pizza alternative!

Cream Cheese Scrambled Eggs

Ingredients:

- 4 large eggs
- 2 tbsp cream cheese, cubed
- 1 tbsp butter
- Salt and pepper to taste
- Fresh chives or parsley for garnish (optional)

Instructions:

1. In a bowl, whisk eggs with salt and pepper until well combined.
2. Heat butter in a skillet over medium heat.
3. Pour in the eggs and cook, stirring occasionally.
4. Add cubed cream cheese to the eggs and stir until the eggs are soft and creamy.
5. Garnish with fresh herbs if desired, and serve hot.

Ground Beef and Zucchini Skillet

Ingredients:

- 1 lb ground beef
- 2 medium zucchinis, diced
- 1 small onion, chopped
- 2 cloves garlic, minced
- 1 tbsp olive oil
- 1 tsp smoked paprika
- ½ tsp cumin
- Salt and pepper to taste

Instructions:

1. Heat olive oil in a large skillet over medium heat.
2. Add ground beef and cook, breaking it apart as it browns.
3. Remove excess fat from the pan, then add onion and garlic. Cook for 3–4 minutes until softened.
4. Add diced zucchini to the skillet and cook for 5–7 minutes until tender.
5. Stir in smoked paprika, cumin, salt, and pepper.
6. Serve hot as a quick and easy meal.

BLT Lettuce Wraps

Ingredients:

- 8 slices bacon, cooked and crispy
- 2 medium tomatoes, sliced
- 1 avocado, sliced (optional)
- 1 head romaine or butter lettuce, leaves separated
- 2 tbsp mayonnaise
- Salt and pepper to taste

Instructions:

1. Lay out large lettuce leaves as a base.
2. Spread a thin layer of mayonnaise on each leaf.
3. Top with 1–2 bacon slices, tomato, and avocado.
4. Sprinkle with salt and pepper.
5. Roll or fold the lettuce into a wrap and serve immediately.

Chicken Alfredo Bake

Ingredients:

- 2 cups cooked shredded chicken
- 1 cup steamed broccoli (optional)
- 1 ½ cups shredded mozzarella
- 1 cup heavy cream
- ½ cup grated Parmesan cheese
- 2 cloves garlic, minced
- Salt and pepper to taste

Instructions:

1. Preheat oven to 375°F (190°C).
2. In a saucepan, combine cream, garlic, and Parmesan; simmer 5 minutes until thick.
3. Mix chicken, broccoli, and Alfredo sauce in a baking dish.
4. Top with mozzarella and bake 15–20 minutes until bubbly and golden.

Zoodle Spaghetti with Meat Sauce

Ingredients:

- 4 medium zucchinis, spiralized
- 1 lb ground beef or turkey
- 2 cups sugar-free marinara sauce
- 1 tbsp olive oil
- 1 tsp Italian seasoning
- Salt and pepper to taste

Instructions:

1. In a skillet, cook ground meat with seasoning until browned. Drain fat.
2. Stir in marinara sauce and simmer 10 minutes.
3. In another skillet, sauté zoodles in olive oil for 2–3 minutes until slightly tender.
4. Serve meat sauce over zoodles.

Broccoli Cheese Soup

Ingredients:

- 4 cups chopped broccoli
- 2 cups chicken or vegetable broth
- 1 cup heavy cream
- 2 cups shredded cheddar cheese
- 1 tbsp butter
- 1 clove garlic, minced
- Salt and pepper to taste

Instructions:

1. In a pot, sauté garlic in butter.
2. Add broccoli and broth; simmer 10 minutes until tender.
3. Stir in cream and cheese. Blend for a smoother texture, or leave chunky.
4. Simmer 5 more minutes, season, and serve hot.

Cauliflower Mac and Cheese

Ingredients:

- 1 head cauliflower, cut into florets
- 1 cup heavy cream
- 2 cups shredded cheddar cheese
- 1 tsp mustard powder
- Salt and pepper to taste

Instructions:

1. Boil cauliflower 5–7 minutes until fork-tender; drain.
2. In a saucepan, simmer cream and mustard powder.
3. Add cheese and stir until melted.
4. Mix cauliflower into the cheese sauce. Serve warm.

Keto Cheeseburger Casserole

Ingredients:

- 1 lb ground beef
- 1 small onion, chopped
- 1 cup shredded cheddar cheese
- 3 eggs
- ½ cup heavy cream
- 1 tbsp mustard
- Pickles for garnish (optional)
- Salt and pepper to taste

Instructions:

1. Preheat oven to 350°F (175°C).
2. Brown beef with onion in a skillet; season with salt and pepper.
3. In a bowl, whisk eggs, cream, and mustard.
4. Place beef in a baking dish, top with cheese, pour egg mixture over.
5. Bake 25 minutes. Top with pickles and serve.

Buffalo Chicken Lettuce Wraps

Ingredients:

- 2 cups shredded cooked chicken
- ¼ cup buffalo sauce
- 1 head butter lettuce
- ¼ cup ranch or blue cheese dressing
- Celery sticks for garnish (optional)

Instructions:

1. Mix chicken with buffalo sauce.
2. Spoon into lettuce leaves.
3. Drizzle with dressing and serve with celery if desired.

Bunless Bacon Cheeseburgers

Ingredients:

- 1 lb ground beef, shaped into patties
- 4 slices cheddar cheese
- 4 slices bacon, cooked
- Lettuce, tomato, pickles for topping
- Salt and pepper to taste

Instructions:

1. Grill or pan-fry burgers to desired doneness.
2. Top with cheese and let melt.
3. Serve on lettuce leaves with bacon and toppings.

Taco-Stuffed Avocados

Ingredients:

- 2 ripe avocados, halved and pitted
- ½ lb ground beef or turkey
- 1 tbsp taco seasoning
- ¼ cup salsa
- ¼ cup shredded cheese
- Sour cream and chopped cilantro for topping

Instructions:

1. Brown meat and add taco seasoning and salsa.
2. Spoon meat into avocado halves.
3. Top with cheese, sour cream, and cilantro.

Pepperoni Pizza Zucchini Boats

Ingredients:

- 3 medium zucchinis, halved and hollowed
- ½ cup marinara sauce
- 1 cup shredded mozzarella
- ¼ cup mini pepperoni or chopped regular
- 1 tsp Italian seasoning

Instructions:

1. Preheat oven to 375°F (190°C).
2. Place zucchini halves on a baking sheet.
3. Spoon sauce into each, top with cheese and pepperoni.
4. Sprinkle with seasoning and bake 15–20 minutes.

Egg Roll in a Bowl

Ingredients:

- 1 lb ground pork or turkey
- 1 bag (12 oz) coleslaw mix
- 2 cloves garlic, minced
- 1 tbsp ginger, grated
- 2 tbsp soy sauce or coconut aminos
- 1 tbsp sesame oil
- Green onions and sesame seeds for garnish

Instructions:

1. In a large skillet, cook meat until browned.
2. Add garlic, ginger, and soy sauce; stir for 1 minute.
3. Add coleslaw mix; cook until wilted, about 5 minutes.
4. Drizzle with sesame oil, stir well.
5. Top with green onions and sesame seeds to serve.

Keto Chicken Salad

Ingredients:

- 2 cups cooked, shredded or chopped chicken
- ⅓ cup mayonnaise
- 1 tbsp Dijon mustard
- 2 celery stalks, finely chopped
- 1 tbsp lemon juice
- Salt, pepper, and paprika to taste

Instructions:

1. Combine all ingredients in a bowl.
2. Mix until fully coated and creamy.
3. Chill before serving in lettuce cups or on its own.

Garlic Butter Shrimp

Ingredients:

- 1 lb shrimp, peeled and deveined
- 3 tbsp butter
- 4 cloves garlic, minced
- 1 tbsp lemon juice
- 1 tbsp chopped parsley
- Salt and pepper to taste

Instructions:

1. In a skillet, melt butter over medium heat.
2. Add garlic; sauté 1 minute.
3. Add shrimp, season, and cook 2–3 minutes per side.
4. Finish with lemon juice and parsley. Serve hot.

Keto Sloppy Joes

Ingredients:

- 1 lb ground beef
- ½ small onion, chopped
- 1 tbsp tomato paste
- ⅓ cup sugar-free ketchup
- 1 tsp mustard
- 1 tbsp Worcestershire sauce
- Salt and pepper to taste

Instructions:

1. Cook beef and onion in a skillet until browned.
2. Stir in tomato paste, ketchup, mustard, and Worcestershire.
3. Simmer 5–10 minutes until thick.
4. Serve over lettuce cups or low-carb bread.

Pork Chop and Green Beans Skillet

Ingredients:

- 2–4 boneless pork chops
- 2 cups green beans, trimmed
- 2 tbsp olive oil
- 2 cloves garlic, minced
- Salt, pepper, and Italian seasoning

Instructions:

1. Season pork chops with salt, pepper, and seasoning.
2. In a skillet, sear chops 4–5 minutes per side. Remove and set aside.
3. In same pan, add garlic and green beans; sauté 5–6 minutes.
4. Return pork to skillet and heat through.

Keto Tuna Melt

Ingredients:

- 1 can tuna, drained
- 2 tbsp mayonnaise
- 1 tbsp chopped pickles or relish
- ¼ cup shredded cheddar cheese
- Salt and pepper
- Optional: use a chaffle or low-carb bread

Instructions:

1. Mix tuna, mayo, pickles, and seasoning.
2. Spoon onto low-carb base and top with cheese.
3. Broil or toast until cheese melts. Serve warm.

Chicken Fajita Bowl

Ingredients:

- 2 chicken breasts, sliced
- 1 bell pepper, sliced
- 1 onion, sliced
- 1 tbsp olive oil
- 1 tbsp fajita seasoning
- Cauliflower rice, avocado, and salsa for serving

Instructions:

1. Toss chicken and veggies with oil and seasoning.
2. Cook in a skillet until chicken is done and veggies are soft.
3. Serve over cauliflower rice with toppings.

Creamy Spinach-Stuffed Chicken

Ingredients:

- 2 large chicken breasts
- ½ cup chopped spinach (fresh or frozen)
- ¼ cup cream cheese
- ¼ cup shredded mozzarella
- 2 tbsp Parmesan
- Salt, pepper, garlic powder

Instructions:

1. Slice a pocket into each chicken breast.
2. Mix spinach, cheeses, and seasoning.
3. Stuff mixture into each chicken breast.
4. Bake at 375°F (190°C) for 25–30 minutes until cooked through.

Keto Egg Muffins

Ingredients:

- 6 eggs
- ¼ cup heavy cream
- ½ cup shredded cheese
- ½ cup chopped veggies (peppers, spinach, onion)
- ½ cup cooked bacon or sausage
- Salt and pepper to taste

Instructions:

1. Preheat oven to 375°F (190°C).
2. Whisk eggs, cream, salt, and pepper.
3. Grease a muffin tin and divide meat, cheese, and veggies evenly.
4. Pour egg mixture on top.
5. Bake 20–25 minutes until set and golden.

Mushroom and Swiss Omelet

Ingredients:

- 3 eggs
- ½ cup mushrooms, sliced
- ¼ cup shredded Swiss cheese
- 1 tbsp butter
- Salt and pepper

Instructions:

1. In a skillet, sauté mushrooms in butter until soft. Remove and set aside.
2. Whisk eggs with salt and pepper, pour into pan.
3. Cook until nearly set, add mushrooms and cheese.
4. Fold and finish cooking. Serve hot.

Hot Dog Lettuce Wraps

Ingredients:

- 4 beef hot dogs
- 4 large lettuce leaves
- Mustard, sugar-free ketchup, or mayo
- Diced onions and pickles (optional)

Instructions:

1. Cook hot dogs by boiling, grilling, or pan-frying.
2. Wrap each in a large lettuce leaf.
3. Add toppings of choice and serve.

Chicken Bacon Ranch Casserole

Ingredients:

- 2 cups cooked, chopped chicken
- ½ cup cooked crumbled bacon
- ½ cup ranch dressing
- 1 cup shredded cheddar cheese
- ½ cup steamed broccoli (optional)

Instructions:

1. Preheat oven to 375°F (190°C).
2. Mix all ingredients in a baking dish.
3. Bake 20–25 minutes until bubbly and golden.

Keto Meatballs

Ingredients:

- 1 lb ground beef
- 1 egg
- ¼ cup grated Parmesan
- 1 tsp Italian seasoning
- 2 cloves garlic, minced
- Salt and pepper

Instructions:

1. Preheat oven to 400°F (200°C).
2. Mix all ingredients in a bowl and form into meatballs.
3. Place on a baking sheet and bake 18–20 minutes.
4. Serve with sugar-free marinara sauce or as-is.

Shrimp and Broccoli Stir-Fry

Ingredients:

- 1 lb shrimp, peeled and deveined
- 2 cups broccoli florets
- 2 tbsp coconut aminos or soy sauce
- 1 tbsp sesame oil
- 1 clove garlic, minced
- Salt and pepper

Instructions:

1. Sauté garlic in sesame oil, add shrimp and cook 2–3 minutes.
2. Add broccoli and soy sauce. Cook until broccoli is tender and shrimp is pink.
3. Serve hot.

Keto Quesadillas (Cheese Shell)

Ingredients:

- 1 ½ cups shredded cheddar or mozzarella
- ½ cup cooked chicken or beef
- Sour cream, salsa, or guacamole for serving

Instructions:

1. Heat a non-stick skillet and spread cheese in a circle.
2. Cook until bubbly and edges brown, then let cool slightly to crisp.
3. Add meat, fold like a quesadilla, and cook 1–2 more minutes.
4. Serve with toppings.

Pepperoni Cheese Crisps

Ingredients:

- 1 cup shredded mozzarella or cheddar
- 20–30 slices of pepperoni

Instructions:

1. Preheat oven to 400°F (200°C).
2. On a parchment-lined baking sheet, place small piles of cheese topped with pepperoni.
3. Bake 7–10 minutes until crispy.
4. Cool before serving for best crunch.

Sausage Egg Casserole

Ingredients:

- 6 eggs
- 1 cup cooked breakfast sausage
- ½ cup shredded cheddar
- ¼ cup heavy cream
- Salt, pepper, and herbs to taste

Instructions:

1. Preheat oven to 375°F (190°C).
2. Whisk eggs, cream, cheese, and seasonings.
3. Stir in sausage and pour into greased baking dish.
4. Bake 25–30 minutes until center is set.

Cobb Salad

Ingredients:

- 2 cups mixed greens
- 1 cup cooked chicken breast, chopped
- 2 boiled eggs, sliced
- ½ avocado, sliced
- ¼ cup blue cheese crumbles
- 2 strips cooked bacon, crumbled
- ½ cup cherry tomatoes, halved
- 2 tbsp olive oil
- 1 tbsp red wine vinegar
- Salt and pepper to taste

Instructions:

1. Arrange the mixed greens on a plate.
2. Add the chicken, eggs, avocado, cheese, bacon, and tomatoes in separate sections.
3. Drizzle with olive oil, vinegar, and season with salt and pepper.
4. Toss before serving.

Keto Chicken Nuggets

Ingredients:

- 1 lb chicken breast, cut into bite-sized pieces
- 1 cup almond flour
- 1 tsp garlic powder
- 1 tsp onion powder
- 1 tsp paprika
- 2 eggs, beaten
- Salt and pepper to taste
- Olive oil for frying

Instructions:

1. Preheat oven to 400°F (200°C).
2. Mix almond flour, garlic powder, onion powder, paprika, salt, and pepper in a bowl.
3. Dip chicken pieces into egg, then coat in the flour mixture.
4. Heat oil in a skillet over medium-high heat and fry nuggets until golden.
5. Place on a baking sheet and bake for 5–7 minutes to ensure they're cooked through.

Cauliflower Tots

Ingredients:

- 1 medium cauliflower, grated
- 1 cup shredded cheddar cheese
- 1 egg
- ½ cup almond flour
- 1 tsp garlic powder
- Salt and pepper to taste
- Olive oil spray

Instructions:

1. Preheat oven to 375°F (190°C).
2. Steam cauliflower until tender, then squeeze out excess moisture.
3. Combine cauliflower, cheese, egg, almond flour, garlic powder, salt, and pepper.
4. Form mixture into small tot shapes and place on a baking sheet.
5. Spray with olive oil and bake for 20–25 minutes until golden.

Chili Dog Casserole

Ingredients:

- 4 beef hot dogs, sliced
- 1 cup sugar-free chili
- 1 cup shredded cheddar cheese
- ½ small onion, chopped
- 1 tbsp olive oil
- Salt and pepper

Instructions:

1. Preheat oven to 375°F (190°C).
2. Sauté onions in olive oil until soft.
3. Add sliced hot dogs and cook for 3–4 minutes.
4. Stir in chili, salt, and pepper.
5. Transfer to a casserole dish, top with cheese, and bake for 15–20 minutes until bubbly.

Pulled Pork Lettuce Wraps

Ingredients:

- 1 lb pork shoulder, cooked and shredded
- ¼ cup sugar-free BBQ sauce
- 8 large lettuce leaves
- Sliced pickles (optional)

Instructions:

1. Shred the cooked pork shoulder with a fork.
2. Toss with BBQ sauce.
3. Scoop the pulled pork onto large lettuce leaves and top with pickles if desired.
4. Roll up and serve.

Greek Salad with Grilled Chicken

Ingredients:

- 2 chicken breasts, grilled and sliced
- 2 cups mixed greens
- ½ cucumber, sliced
- ½ cup cherry tomatoes, halved
- ¼ red onion, thinly sliced
- ¼ cup Kalamata olives
- ¼ cup feta cheese
- 2 tbsp olive oil
- 1 tbsp lemon juice
- 1 tsp dried oregano
- Salt and pepper to taste

Instructions:

1. Arrange greens, cucumber, tomatoes, onion, olives, and feta on a plate.
2. Top with sliced grilled chicken.
3. Drizzle with olive oil, lemon juice, and season with oregano, salt, and pepper.
4. Toss and serve.

Keto Chicken Stir-Fry

Ingredients:

- 1 lb chicken breast, sliced thin
- 2 tbsp coconut oil
- 1 bell pepper, sliced
- 1 zucchini, sliced
- 1 cup broccoli florets
- 2 tbsp soy sauce or coconut aminos
- 1 tbsp sesame oil
- 1 tsp ginger, minced
- 1 clove garlic, minced
- Salt and pepper to taste

Instructions:

1. Heat coconut oil in a large skillet or wok over medium-high heat.
2. Add chicken and cook until browned.
3. Add vegetables, ginger, and garlic. Stir-fry for 5–7 minutes until vegetables are tender.
4. Stir in soy sauce and sesame oil. Cook for an additional 2 minutes.
5. Season with salt and pepper to taste and serve.

Philly Cheesesteak Stuffed Peppers

Ingredients:

- 4 large bell peppers, tops cut off and seeds removed
- 1 lb ground beef or thinly sliced steak
- 1 onion, sliced
- 1 bell pepper, sliced
- 1 cup shredded provolone or mozzarella cheese
- 2 tbsp olive oil
- Salt and pepper to taste
- 1 tbsp Worcestershire sauce (optional)

Instructions:

1. Preheat oven to 375°F (190°C).
2. Sauté onions and sliced bell peppers in olive oil until softened.
3. Add ground beef or steak, season with salt, pepper, and Worcestershire sauce. Cook until browned.
4. Stuff the peppers with the meat mixture.
5. Top with shredded cheese and bake for 15–20 minutes until peppers are tender and cheese is melted.

Bacon-Wrapped Asparagus

Ingredients:

- 1 bunch of asparagus, trimmed
- 12 slices bacon
- Salt and pepper to taste
- Olive oil (optional)

Instructions:

1. Preheat oven to 400°F (200°C).
2. Wrap 3–4 asparagus spears in a slice of bacon.
3. Place bacon-wrapped asparagus on a baking sheet.
4. Drizzle with olive oil if desired and season with salt and pepper.
5. Bake for 20–25 minutes until bacon is crispy and asparagus is tender.

Turkey and Cheese Roll-Ups

Ingredients:

- 8 slices deli turkey breast
- 4 oz cream cheese, softened
- ½ cup shredded cheddar cheese
- 1 tbsp mustard or mayonnaise
- Salt and pepper to taste

Instructions:

1. Spread cream cheese and mustard or mayo on each slice of turkey.
2. Sprinkle with cheddar cheese and season with salt and pepper.
3. Roll up the turkey slices and secure with toothpicks.
4. Serve as is or refrigerate for 30 minutes before serving for extra firmness.

Keto Deviled Eggs

Ingredients:

- 6 large eggs, hard-boiled
- ¼ cup mayonnaise
- 1 tbsp Dijon mustard
- 1 tsp vinegar
- Salt and pepper to taste
- Paprika for garnish (optional)

Instructions:

1. Peel the hard-boiled eggs and slice in half.
2. Scoop out the yolks and place in a bowl.
3. Mash yolks with mayonnaise, mustard, vinegar, salt, and pepper until smooth.
4. Spoon or pipe the yolk mixture back into the egg whites.
5. Garnish with paprika if desired and serve.

Spinach and Feta Stuffed Chicken

Ingredients:

- 2 boneless, skinless chicken breasts
- ½ cup cooked spinach, drained and chopped
- ¼ cup crumbled feta cheese
- 2 tbsp cream cheese, softened
- 1 tsp garlic powder
- Salt and pepper to taste
- Olive oil for cooking

Instructions:

1. Preheat oven to 375°F (190°C).
2. Mix spinach, feta, cream cheese, garlic powder, salt, and pepper in a bowl.
3. Slice a pocket into each chicken breast and stuff with the spinach mixture.
4. Heat olive oil in a skillet over medium-high heat and sear chicken on both sides until browned.
5. Transfer chicken to a baking dish and bake for 20–25 minutes until cooked through.

Caprese Chicken Skillet

Ingredients:

- 2 chicken breasts
- 2 tbsp olive oil
- 1 cup cherry tomatoes, halved
- 1 ball fresh mozzarella, sliced
- 2 tbsp balsamic vinegar
- Fresh basil for garnish
- Salt and pepper to taste

Instructions:

1. Season chicken breasts with salt and pepper.
2. Heat olive oil in a skillet over medium heat and cook chicken for 6–7 minutes per side until golden and cooked through.
3. Add cherry tomatoes to the skillet and sauté for 2–3 minutes.
4. Place mozzarella slices on top of chicken and let melt for 2 minutes.
5. Drizzle with balsamic vinegar and garnish with fresh basil before serving.

www.ingramcontent.com/pod-product-compliance
Lightning Source LLC
LaVergne TN
LVHW081326060526
838201LV00055B/2488